CONVERSATIONS ON THE **GO**

clever questions to keep teens and grown-ups <u>talking</u>

A **SEARCH INSTITUTE** PUBLICATION

BY
MARY ALICE
ACKERMAN

Conversations on the Go
*Clever Questions to Keep Teens and
Grown-Ups Talking*

Mary Alice Ackerman
Copyright © 2004 by Search Institute

The following are trademarks of Search
Institute: Healthy Communities • Healthy
Youth®, Search Institute℠, and Developmental
Assets™.

ISBN-13: 978-1-57482-863-4
ISBN-10: 1-57482-863-0

10 9 8 7 6
Printed on acid-free paper in the United
States of America.

Search Institute
615 First Avenue Northeast, Suite 125
Minneapolis, MN 55413
www.search-institute.org
612-376-8955 • 800-888-7828

CREDITS
Editor: Rebecca Aldridge
Design: Jeanne Lee
Production Coordinator: Mary Ellen Buscher

Library of Congress
Cataloging-in-Publication Data

Ackerman, Mary Alice.
Conversations on the go : clever questions to
keep teens and grown-ups talking /
by Mary Alice Ackerman.
    p. cm.
ISBN 1-57482-863-0 (pbk. : alk. paper)
1. Conversation. 2. Teenagers and adults.
3. Interpersonal relations in adolescence.
I. Title.
BJ2121.A55 2004
649'.7--dc22   2004015239

ABOUT THIS BOOK
Search Institute's Healthy Communities •
Healthy Youth® initiative seeks to unite
individuals, organizations, and their leaders
to join together in nurturing competent,
caring, and responsible children and
adolescents. Lutheran Brotherhood, now
Thrivent Financial for Lutherans, was
the founding national sponsor for Healthy
Communities • Healthy Youth. Thrivent
Financial for Lutherans Foundation has
provided Search Institute with generous
support.

For my friend **Laura Lee Geraghty**

and for my conversation teachers—

Jim and **Jean**

Nils and **Ree**

CONTENTS

conversation is an art.

Ralph Waldo Emerson

Have you ever asked the teen in your life how school was going only to get the response "Fine"? You may try again with "So, what did you learn?" and the answer is "Nothing." From there, the conversation goes even further downhill. If this is your experience, please know that you are not alone! Of course, a day in a teen's life holds much more than this exchange would lead us to believe. Asking a few interesting questions can sometimes bring out the stories that remain hidden.

This book gives all of us permission to ask some of the questions that open a window into the hearts and minds of young people and help us connect with them.

And we need to connect. According to data from Search Institute in Minneapolis, only 1 in 4 adolescents finds parents approachable and available to talk. Experts say that developmentally responsive family environments are those in which parents are aware of the joys and concerns of their children and are willing to engage in meaningful, open communication about those issues. The questions in this book can provide the first step on a path toward open communication between adults and teens.

How to Use This Book

You can use this book anytime, anyplace. Take it with you in the car when driving to sports practice. Bring it along on the plane or car ride when taking a family vacation. Leave the book nearby on the kitchen table to dig into and linger over during meals. Open it up during a family meeting. Whisper questions and answers to each other while waiting in a doctor's office. Pull it out while riding the bus. Share it with grandparents to help them stay on top of their grandchildren's fast-changing lives. If you're a mentor or youth leader, use these questions to open up better dialogues. Get creative and write in your own questions. Encourage brothers and sisters to ask each other the questions—hopefully within your earshot. Let the young people in your life turn the tables and ask you the questions!

There is no one right way to use this book. I divided the book into the eight asset categories that make up the Developmental Assets framework. (You can read more about the Developmental Assets in the last chapter of this book. For now, just know that the more "assets" young people have, the *more likely* they are to engage in healthy behaviors and the *less likely* they are to be involved in risky activities.) Start at the beginning with Support and work your way through to Positive Identity, if you'd like. Or mix it up. For example, you might:

- Try finding a question that relates to something you are curious about and start there;

- Hand the book to the young person and let her or him choose a question she or he feels like talking about; or

- Open the book and choose a question at random.

As I said, there isn't just one right way to use this book. The object is to talk with each other and have some fun!

Getting over the Hurdles

Many adults find that talking with teens is "so hard," maybe even "scary." Is it that young people look different than we did at their age? Is it that teenagers are so busy asserting their independence that we believe they don't need or want us in their lives any more? Have we forgotten how important some adults were to us at their age?

This may surprise many adults, but the teenagers I talked with when writing this book actually said they wanted more connection with adults. These young people know they look different, but they also believe they are not so different inside. They hoped this book would give adults permission to start conversations.

Adult friends who were not parents or whose children were long "out of the nest" had their own reaction. These adults felt very disconnected from young people. They felt there was no role for them with today's youth. Some said they felt the only way to connect with youth was through formal programs that were tough to fit into their busy schedules. As we talked further, they realized that there were hidden opportunities for conversations—with the neighbor's child or with a niece or nephew who lives out of town, for example. It was eye-opening for them to hear that young people would welcome more connection to the adults in their midst.

Since working in the field of adolescent development, I have become more courageous about starting conversations with young people I don't really know—young people such as Matt, who bags groceries at my grocery store, or the young girl, Shauna, who makes my lattés at the coffee shop. I can tell by the smiles of recognition when they see me coming that we are connected. Every caring, responsible adult with whom young people connect makes them stronger. Really.

Begin making your own connections by telling the young person you are hoping to engage that you would like to get to know her or him better. You can let the young person know that you want to make more time to simply talk. You may be surprised by how flattered he or she might feel. Making time for that person alone means a lot. The first few times you pick up this book, the conversations may feel a bit awkward or unnatural—

for both of you! But you will soon get over that first hurdle and be well on your way to great conversations.

Tips for Making Conversation Work

KEEP IT GOING. It's one thing to ask a question and sit back for the answer. It is another thing to really engage in a conversation. Asking follow-up questions or providing open-ended responses are great ways to keep the conversation going. This list shares some old standbys:

> "That's interesting. Tell me more."
> "You've really thought about this, haven't you?"
> "Have you always thought this way?"
> "Are you saying . . . ?
> "Interesting. Have you thought about . . . ?"
> "What experience led you to feel this way?"

Please remember, the idea is not to debate an answer but to learn more. Acknowledging a young person's opinion as valid, even if you don't think it is "right," shows respect. As a result, you model tolerance and being nonjudgmental. And you probably know this, but it's worth a reminder: belittling an answer or telling young people they are "wrong" will make the next conversation pretty tough to start.

CONVERSATION DOESN'T HAVE TO BE "HEAVY." It is important to have conversations about subjects that matter deeply, such as who are the most influential people in a young person's life. It is also important to listen to why a young person likes a current fad, music star, or TV program. All conversations are meaningful when two people are truly engaged and interested in one another's questions and answers.

BE PREPARED FOR THE UNEXPECTED ANSWER. You may ask a question and get an answer you did not want or expect. Remember, the object in asking these questions is to be engaged, not to prove a point or win an argument or teach a lesson. If an answer bothers you (perhaps it doesn't reflect the values you hoped for), simply listen and ask more questions about why the young person thinks and feels that way. Suspend your own judgment and let young people express their ideas and opinions.

When I feel the need to respond to something my child shares in a way other than would be constructive, I carefully consider my response and reframe it if necessary. Sometimes I buy time with questions such as "What makes you believe that?" or "Could you tell me more?" These responses help me to avoid judging right away. I learn a bit more about what makes my granddaughter tick, and I gain more insight into the person she is becoming.

If the answer still bothers me a day or two later, it's a great opportunity to say, "Remember how you responded to that question yesterday? I need to talk some more"—a set-up for another conversation!

LISTENING IS MOST IMPORTANT. Conversations with kids are better when we adults carefully practice the art of listening. Through careful listening we tell them we care about their thoughts—we care about them. When I talk with young people, I also have to try very hard not to judge them, not to tell them the answers, not to give my opinion—unless it is asked for. I simply *listen.*

TIMING CAN BE EVERYTHING. Young people tell me that they sometimes feel as if their whole day at school is filled with adults asking them questions. If you ask a question that is met with silence or "the look," maybe this isn't the best time for a conversation. Or it could be that a question triggers a bigger issue for them, and they need some time to process it. Taking a rain check on a question is okay.

ASK THE SAME QUESTION AGAIN. You can ask the same question several weeks or years apart and get very different answers. It is a great way for you to watch a young person's developmental growth.

ENJOY THE EXCHANGE! Our kids are very wise. By intentionally engaging in conversations with them, we can learn a lot. Listen for their convictions and passions. Support their newly forming independence. And be prepared to have the tables turned on you. Kids wonder about who we are under our adult exteriors, too!

<u>Making Connections</u>

Conversations are really about creating and maintaining relationships. I work for Search Institute, a not-for-profit organization that conducts research around the activities and traits that help young people succeed. We call these attributes *Developmental Assets*. One of the ways we adults can help the young people in our lives build these assets is to intentionally engage them in conversations—lots of them, about all kinds of things, any chance we get.

Building assets for and with young people is not just about parents and their children; it is about all adults and all kids. What we know through our research is that the more caring adults young people have in their lives, the stronger and more successful they will be. This means that you can have a huge impact on *all* the young people with whom you come in contact. So don't be shy—invite the young people in your life to join you for some conversation. Just grab the book and go!

TALKING ABOUT
SUPPORT
♥

Name
a relative of yours
that you admire.
What makes this person
admirable?

What was
the nicest compliment
you ever received
from an adult?

Tell about your <u>favorite teacher</u>.

16

What was your **first memory** as a little child?

How would you <u>work to end violence in schools</u> if you had the authority to do it?

What is your <u>favorite family tradition</u>?

Do you think it's hard for **young people and adults** to communicate? What could adults and young people do to improve communication?

Who are the **three people** in your life you know you can always count on? Why did you choose them?

What <u>school activity</u> do you most wish you could be a part of? What holds you back?

What is the **most important quality** you look for in a friend?

How many **nicknames** have you been given? What is your favorite?

What **questions** would you like adults to ask you or your friends?

Which <u>adults in your life</u> have helped you become who you are? What did they do?

Are any **parents** of your friends "cool"? What makes a parent "cool"?

What **two questions** do you have about your family history?

2

**Do you have friends who are going through
<u>tough times</u> or whose families are not supportive?
What do you and your friends do to support them?**

What's the
best advice
an adult ever gave
you? What's the
worst?

**<u>What makes a neighborhood feel like a caring place?</u>
If you could make one change to make
your neighborhood a more caring place to grow up,
what would it be?**

FEEL FREE TO CHANGE ANY QUESTION.

What is **one of the best talks** you remember having with a family member?

Who is your **favorite nonfamous adult?** Why?

If you could <u>change just one thing</u> about your school to make it a more caring place, what would it be? How can adults and young people make that change happen?

What's the **most pressing issue** at your school right now?

If <u>your neighborhood</u> could join together for a cause, what would you like that cause to be?

Who would you talk to if you were feeling pressured to do something that you didn't want to do? Why would you choose this person?

What is something or someone you **loved, but lost?**

Talk about a time <u>when you laughed so hard</u> you thought you couldn't stop.

Who is **your favorite neighbor** and why?

How well do the **students in your school** get along?

RESPECT

What does the word <u>respect</u> mean to peers at your school? to teachers at your school?

What was the **best gift** you ever received?

TALKING ABOUT **EMPOWERMENT**

Have you ever seen **someone bullying** someone else? Did you step in or not?

How important is it to vote in elections in today's world? Are there ways you and your friends could have an impact on elections now?

Name something you have always wished you could do. How could you make it happen?

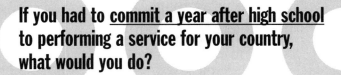

If you had to <u>commit a year after high school</u> to performing a service for your country, what would you do?

Talk about a time when an **adult** treated you as an **equal**.

Do you think **your community** is a good place to grow up? Describe what tells you that.

27

How would **school be different** if kids made and enforced the rules?

How much **work** or how many **chores** should each person in your family do to make the household run smoothly? How would you assign the work?

Name <u>someone younger than you</u> who looks up to you. How do you know that he or she looks up to you?

Talk about a time when you felt really <u>strong and competent</u>.

How easy is it to talk about **serious issues** with your friends?

Have you ever felt as if someone **discriminated** against you? How did you deal with it, or how would you deal with it now?

Was there ever a time at school when you feared for **your own safety**? What was the situation, and what did you do?

Name **four things** you like best about yourself.

Have you ever done a <u>good deed</u> for someone without them knowing it was you? What could you do this week for someone?

What are you most **fearful** of?

What's the biggest way someone has made a positive difference in your life?

Complete this sentence: One way I'd like to **change the world** is . . .

Talk about a situation that showed you that **you matter to others.**

Who asks you for <u>opinions and advice</u>? What are some of the things you tell them?

If you could be **any superhero**, which one would you be and why? What would you do with your powers?

What are the <u>best places</u> to hang out in your community? If you could create the perfect hangout, what would you include?

Name the **talents** of each person in your family.

Do most adults have <u>positive</u> or <u>negative</u> views of teenagers? How could you let them know who you really are?

What are the
worst problems
in the world today that
you wish you could do
something about?

Who protects you?
Who looks to you for protection?

Do you believe
there is **too much
pressure** on
kids today?

What would you like **other family members** to teach you?

Tell about a time when you wanted to <u>stand up for something</u> or someone, but you were afraid to. What would you do differently now?

Do you think there is more **good** or **evil** in the world? What makes you believe that?

TALKING ABOUT

BOUNDARIES & EXPECTATIONS

How do you feel when someone pushes you to do **your best?**

Are the **rules** at school **fair?** Which rules would you change and why?

What would you do if you saw two students <u>cheating on a test?</u> Is there a "right" thing to do?

What **special qualities** should a role model have?

Do you have friends whose family rules are *too* strict? Why do you consider them too strict? Do you have friends whose family rules should be more strict? Why?

Think about the **neighborhoods** where your friends live. Is there one you would move to if you could? Why would it be better?

What do you do **when you disagree** with rules you are supposed to follow?

What are **three things** about you that your friends would say make you a good friend to have?

Talk about a time when you <u>really succeeded</u> at something and surprised yourself.

Have you ever had a friend whom you later realized was a "<u>bad influence</u>" on you? How did you handle it?

Do some
family rules
actually help you say
no when friends ask
you to do something
that you don't
want to do?

In what
ways do you
wish you had more
freedom?

If you could describe <u>your ideal day,</u> what would it be like?

Which friend
makes you feel best about yourself? How does he or she do that?

Would you rather live in the
country, a tiny rural town, a suburb of a city, or an urban city center? Why?

Have you ever found yourself **not going along** with the crowd? Why did you choose that route?

What's the <u>biggest mistake</u> you've made so far in your life? What did you learn from it?

<u>Which teacher, coach, or other school worker</u> is a positive role model for you?
What qualities do you value in her or him?

How does **trust** get broken? Can trust be repaired?

What is your **highest expectation** for yourself?

Which <u>family rules</u> do you most wish you could change? What are your reasons?

Do you think there's a good part to **making mistakes?** Why or why not?

<u>**Have you ever been in a situation**</u> **where someone dared someone else to do something you all know is wrong? What was the situation? If it happened again tomorrow, what would you do?**

If you could make **three rules** for parents, what would they be? Why?

Who makes a better role model:
someone famous or someone not famous?
What are your reasons for thinking this?

Are there consistent family, school, and neighborhood **boundaries** in your life? Does this make life easier or harder?

Why do you think adults set **curfews** for teenagers?

What is your biggest dream?
What is the first step you can take toward achieving it?

Do you think you are a **role model** for anyone? Why or why not?

What's the <u>best story</u> you've ever heard about someone overcoming an obstacle?

TALKING ABOUT

CONSTRUCTIVE USE OF TIME

If someone told you that you could start **a new club** or program at school, what would it be?

<u>Do you believe in a higher power or "God"?</u>
How do you know there is or is not one?
Has your opinion changed on this?

When you spend time at home, what is
<u>your favorite thing to do</u>? How could you arrange
to do more of it?

What is the **silliest thing** you've ever done in public?

How does <u>being on a team</u> — sports, clubs, study groups — help you when you become an adult?

Think back on all the **art** you have created. Is there one picture, pot, sculpture you are most proud of?

Who is your **favorite musician?** What do you like about her or his music?

If you could go to the <u>Olympic games</u> on any team, what sport would you choose and why?

What is your favorite **family time** together?

Do you think it's important to have separation between **church** and **state?**

Good artists say they learned to excel at their craft by spending time **practicing.** Describe a time when practice paid off for you.

Is there a religion or belief system that you are curious about? What would you like to learn?

If you have to choose between doing activities <u>inside</u> or doing activities <u>outside</u>, which do you do? Do you think you have a balance?

What was the last time you were in a **leadership** position? Were you an effective leader?

If you could be a <u>professional artist</u>, which would you be: a painter, dancer, singer, actor, sculptor, craftsperson, or writer? Why?

What **activities** do you do to make the world a better place?

Who or what do you turn to when you want <u>spiritual guidance</u> or help with an important problem?

home

When do you feel that you need to get away from **home?** When is home an escape for you?

WWW.

What are your favorite types of **Web sites** to visit? Why?

Do you spend most of your time <u>playing</u> or <u>working</u>? How could you create more balance?

What is your definition of **faith** or **spirituality?**

Are you sometimes afraid to <u>try new things</u> because you think you won't be good at them? How could you encourage yourself more?

If you could **take lessons** in anything, what would you learn?

How could you **share your talents** with the community?

What is the best thing <u>television</u> has done for our world? What is the worst thing?

Would you rather spend your time at a **history, science, or art museum?** Why?

How do the **activities** you do teach you more about yourself? What have you learned?

Is it important to know <u>a person's religion</u> when deciding whether to be friends? Why or why not? What about when deciding to date a person?

How do you know when someone is spending too much time **watching TV** or **playing video games?**

Do you believe in **ghosts** or **evil spirits?** Would you stay alone in a house that people said was haunted?

TALKING ABOUT

COMMITMENT TO LEARNING

What do you say if someone asks how you're doing in school? How do you know if you're doing well?

What was your **favorite book** when you were young? What did you like about it?

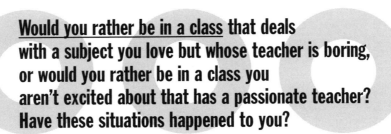

Would you rather be in a class that deals with a subject you love but whose teacher is boring, or would you rather be in a class you aren't excited about that has a passionate teacher? Have these situations happened to you?

Describe a time when you gave something your best shot, and it still wasn't good enough. Why is it important to give something your best?

What was your **most embarrassing moment** in grade school? in middle school? in high school?

In your school, are young people pushed too hard to succeed or not hard enough?

What is your
**favorite place
to study?**
What do you like
about it?

**Of all your classes this term,
which one will help you most in the <u>real world</u>?**

What was
your **favorite
childhood song?**
Can you still
sing it?

Can you name a time when an outside speaker came to your school and left a lasting impression on you? What was the message he or she delivered?

What is the hardest part of school this year? Is it homework? getting assignments in on time? tests? class participation? getting along with classmates? What makes this hard?

Have you ever asked a teacher or coach for extra help? Was it difficult to ask?

What is a **subject** or **topic** that isn't taught in your school, but you would really like to learn about?

Do your friends work really hard to do well in school, or do they just "get by"?
How does their attitude affect how well you do in school?

If a child asked you, "**Why do I need to go to school?**" how would you respond?

<u>What's the way that you learn best?</u>
Do you like to see something,
read about it,
do it,
hear it,
or practice it?
How can you find out more about
your learning style?

What **school project** have you completed that you're most proud of?

Who most affects your **attitude** toward school?

What's the **best lesson** you've ever learned from a book?

How could your school <u>make you feel more included</u> in decision making? Do you want to help make decisions that affect your school?

What makes a teacher a **good teacher?**

If your friends asked you to <u>name three books</u> they should read, which ones would you recommend? Why would you recommend them?

What helps you do your best with **homework?**

<u>Who at school</u> looks forward to seeing you every day? Can you name at least one adult and one peer?

1 What's your **first memory** of school?

Does your school **honor other achievers** besides athletes? Is it important to do so?

Have you ever thought about <u>dropping out</u> of school? Why or why not?

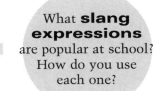
What **slang expressions** are popular at school? How do you use each one?

<u>Can you recite</u> a poem, song verse, or nursery rhyme?

If there was one school year you would <u>NEVER</u> do again, which one would it be? Why?

TALKING ABOUT
POSITIVE VALUES

Was there ever a time when you had to <u>stand up for something you believed</u> even when your friends weren't behind you 100 percent? What was it, and what did you learn from the experience?

What **four qualities** will you look for in a life partner?

Is there such a thing as a **"good" war?**

When you die and people are talking about your life, what do you hope they say about you?

<u>Who is the nicest person you know?</u>
What qualities or actions make you think of her or him that way? Do you think a person can be *too* nice, too selfless?

Are you good at **keeping secrets?**

Can a person be <u>completely honest</u> at all times?
Is it ever okay to lie?
If so, when is it okay to lie?

Do you think adults give youth enough responsibility? In what areas could young people take more responsibility in their communities? Can youth be given too much responsibility?

equal rights

Is it possible to have a world in which everyone has **equal rights?** What would it take to get there?

How hard or easy is it for you to admit when you are wrong? Has this changed over time?

Who do you choose to talk with when you need to make tough decisions about which way to live your life? Who has been there for you?

What are the benefits of being **responsible?**

What messages do you get about <u>sex and alcohol or other drugs</u> from TV programs, movies, and video games? What messages do you get from friends, teachers, and parents?

Was there ever a time when you had to **tell the truth** even though it was hard? What was the result of telling the truth?

Complete the sentence: **I think it's important** to take the time to help others because . . .

Talk about
the last time someone
encouraged
you.

Have you
ever been affected
by **racism** or
sexism? What
happened and how did
it affect you?

Are there any people <u>it's hard for you</u> to accept and respect? What about them makes them difficult to accept and respect?

sight

How do you react if someone doesn't agree with what you believe?

hearing

touch

Do you ever **avoid helping** another person? Why or why not?

smell

Which sense is the most important: sight, hearing, touch, smell, or taste? Why?

taste

How do you handle the situation when someone lies to you?

Does **equality** mean everyone has to be the same?

What is your **favorite motto** to live by? What are some of your favorite quotations?

How old should people be,
according to the law, before they drink alcohol?
How old should a person be
before he or she is sexually active?

What is
the **biggest
problem** facing
your generation?

Do you think
girls show caring
more than **boys?**
What makes you
think this?

Which **three social issues** most concern you?

How widespread is <u>cheating</u> in schools today?
What makes kids resist cheating?

What does **integrity** mean to you?

TALKING ABOUT

SOCIAL COMPETENCIES

Which has more impact: giving **money** to charities or giving **time** to charities?

At your school, what does it mean to be "<u>popular</u>"? What are the good and bad parts of being popular?

<u>Who is your best friend?</u>
What are her or his three best qualities?

Talk about the last time you had to tell someone you were sorry. Was it easy or hard? Why?

Is it easier to be a **girl** or a **boy?** Why?

Who was your first **boyfriend** or **girlfriend?** Describe her or him.

answer.

"

Have you ever gone through a <u>difficult time</u> with a friend? What was going on, and how did you resolve the situation?

If you could **invent a holiday,** what would it be? What traditions would it include?

Where does **hate** come from? Is it possible to overcome it?

What are
the **five top
qualities** of a
good friend?

How do you
actively work on
being healthy?
Physically?
Mentally?
Emotionally?

People say that <u>writing down a goal</u> is a powerful step
toward making it happen. Do you think
that is true? What goals would you write down?

Do you think adults judge young people who have tattoos, nose rings, or purple hair? How could this change?

Are there enough <u>activities to do on the weekends</u> for kids who don't want to be involved with tobacco, alcohol, and other drugs? What could be done to improve the situation?

What have you learned through your **friendships?** friends

Do you think you are more able or less able than your peers to resist <u>risky behavior</u>? Why are you that way?

Who was your first real **friend?**

Part of being a **parent** is talking with your children about risky behaviors. What is the best way for adults to talk with kids about this stuff?

Have you ever had to <u>defend one of your beliefs</u> to your friends? What was it about? How did it feel to defend yourself?

What makes you **angry?** When you are angry, how do you show it? Is this healthy or unhealthy?

What is one thing about your **cultural heritage** that you are really proud of?

Have you ever felt **rejected** by a friend? If you have, how did you handle the rejection? Do you still think about it?

Name **three things** you really, really believe in that might surprise people.

How do you stay friends with people when you have disagreements or <u>differences of opinion</u>?

Do you try to imagine how other people will feel when deciding on an action to take?

<u>Why does planning matter</u>, when so many things happen unexpectedly? Does planning sometimes get in the way of having fun?

What are the **top three pressures** facing you now?

What are **three creative ways** to say no to peer pressure?

Which of your **friends** do you **most want to be like?** Why?

<u>Are you comfortable</u> around people who are different from you? Why or why not?

POSITIVE IDENTITY

What
are you most
proud
of?

**What does it take to be a leader?
Do you think you are a leader?
Who do you think is a good leader?**

**When
people first
meet you,** what
do you think they
see? What do you
wish they would see
in you?

What is the **bravest thing** you have ever done?

If you could <u>change lives with someone</u>, who would it be? Why?

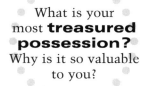

What is your most **treasured possession?** Why is it so valuable to you?

87

If you could change one thing about yourself, what would it be?
How would that change affect your life?

What is the **greatest challenge** you have ever faced? How did you handle it?

Name **three things** that made you smile today.

What are **five words** people would use to describe **you?** What words would you use?

If you could ask any four people to dinner to have great conversations, who would you ask and why?

What will your life be like when you are 30 years old?

What makes you **proud** of your family members?

**<u>When you feel really sad or depressed,
what is the one thing you know will help cheer you up?</u>**

vision

Do you have a **vision** for the person you want to become?

What stresses you out the most? How do you deal with it?

If you could be any **animal,** what would you be? Why?

What do you need in life to be a **truly happy person?**

Have you changed as a person during this past year? How and why?

How do you know your life has a **purpose?** Do you get to choose this purpose, or is the purpose something you're supposed to discover?

How often do you have doubts about yourself?

What is the **trait you most like** about each member of your family?

If you could achieve only one great thing in your life, what would it be?

1

Who needs **you?**

What's the one thing that worries you the most about your future?

What would you rather do: give a speech in front of 200 people or parachute from a plane?

Do you have a **bad habit?** What is it, and how might you break it?

What does it mean to have **personal power?** Are you born with it, or do you grow it, or gather it, or discover it in yourself?

You fast forward **50 years** and discover a new holiday is named in your honor. What would people be celebrating?

What actions are you taking now to make the world better <u>in the future</u>?

About the Developmental Assets

I wrote this book because I have been influenced by a framework called the *Developmental Assets*. This framework is made up of 40 commonsense, positive experiences and qualities that young people need to be successful. You can think about assets as "nutrients" that are necessary for a child to grow a strong mind and character.

Simply but powerfully, assets build the "good stuff" in kids and help them resist the "bad stuff." In our research at Search Institute, we have found that the more assets young people have, the more likely they are to be leaders in their communities, succeed in school, and maintain good health—all traits we want for our kids. Just as importantly, the more assets our children have, the more likely they are to resist risky behavior, such as using alcohol or other drugs, skipping school, or fighting.

Assets don't just happen as part of growing up. They are built for and with children through all of the caring relationships they have at home and in their communities. Family members, teachers, coaches, youth directors, neighbors, and bosses all have opportunities to help make young people stronger. Now you see why having conversations with kids becomes so important: Conversations are the foundation of strong relationships.

The 40 assets are grouped into two main types: external and internal assets. The external assets are the good things young people get from the world around them. The internal assets are the traits, behaviors, and values that help kids make positive choices and be better prepared for challenging situations. Internal assets are like the internal compass that helps guide them.

These two types of assets are divided into eight categories of human development that make it a bit easier to think about activities that can build them. Here are the categories:

EXTERNAL ASSETS

Support is about youth having people and places that make them feel cared about and welcome.

Empowerment is about young people feeling valued for who they are and being given opportunities to shine. It's also about feeling safe, because it is tough to be your best if you feel scared.

Boundaries and Expectations are about knowing and understanding the rules of behavior in families, schools, and communities. They are also about adults and peers encouraging young people to be their best.

Constructive Use of Time is about young people having people and activities in their lives that are fun *and* challenging. It is also about having high-quality time at home.

INTERNAL ASSETS

Commitment to Learning is about doing well in school, but it is also about taking advantage of all opportunities to learn wherever they happen.

Positive Values define who young people are and how they interact with others. These are pretty basic and cover such qualities as honesty, integrity, and knowing how to resolve conflicts peacefully.

Social Competencies are about getting along with all kinds of people and being able to navigate through the rough waters of decision making in today's society.

Positive Identity is about youth feeling good about themselves and knowing they can succeed in life. It's about looking forward to the future.

Search Institute has surveyed thousands of young people over the last decade. What we have found is that, on average, students report having only about 19 of the assets in their lives. That means they have fewer than half of the nutrients that would make them strong. *Fewer than half.* We adults have the power and the responsibility to help all young people in our midst build assets, not just our own children or those in our immediate family. By choosing to engage in meaningful conversations, we begin to intentionally build assets.

ABOUT **SEARCH INSTITUTE**

Search Institute[SM] is an independent, nonprofit, nonsectarian organization whose mission is to provide leadership, knowledge, and resources to promote healthy children, youth, and communities. The institute collaborates with others to promote long-term organizational and cultural change that supports its mission. For a free information packet, call 800-888-7828.

To learn more about Developmental Assets, visit the Search Institute Web site at **www.search-institute.org**.